So What

ALSO BY FREDERICK SEIDEL

Frederick Seidel Selected Poems

Peaches Goes It Alone

Widening Income Inequality

Nice Weather

Poems 1959–2009

Evening Man

Ooga-Booga

The Cosmos Trilogy

Barbados

Area Code 212

Life on Earth

The Cosmos Poems

Going Fast

My Tokyo

These Days

Poems, 1959–1979

Sunrise

Final Solutions

So What

[POEMS]

Frederick Seidel

FARRAR, STRAUS AND GIROUX

NEW YORK

Farrar, Straus and Giroux
120 Broadway, New York 10271

Copyright © 2024 by Frederick Seidel
All rights reserved
Printed in the United States of America
First edition, 2024

Library of Congress Cataloging-in-Publication Data
Names: Seidel, Frederick, 1936– author.
Title: So what : [poems] / Frederick Seidel.
Description: First. | New York : Farrar, Straus and Giroux, 2024.
Identifiers: LCCN 2023051895 | ISBN 9780374614188 (hardcover)
Subjects: LCGFT: Poetry.
Classification: LCC PS3569.E5 S6 2024 | DDC 811/.54—dc23/
    eng/20231106
LC record available at https://lccn.loc.gov/2023051895

Designed by Gretchen Achilles

Our books may be purchased in bulk for promotional,
educational, or business use. Please contact your local bookseller
or the Macmillan Corporate and Premium Sales Department at
1-800-221-7945, extension 5442, or by email at
MacmillanSpecialMarkets@macmillan.com.

www.fsgbooks.com
Follow us on social media at @fsgbooks

1   3   5   7   9   10   8   6   4   2

TO MICHAEL LEONARD

CONTENTS

So What

SO WHAT

I like my coffee sweet so what,
Four sugars to the cup.
I like tea sandwiches at Claridge's,
A plate of perfect with the crust trimmed off.
I like to look out on Brook Street
From rooms on the Brook Street side.
From there I walk to my nearby tailor
And my nearby shotgun maker.

Face the truth.
Poetry doesn't matter in the least.
But, as to *Purdey* poetry, a fabulous new Purdey
28-bore Over-and-Under
Shotgun shoots quail with delicate puffs of thunder
While singing always beautiful
Springtime Christmas carols
Through its beautiful London barrels.

There's nothing on earth as beautiful as a Purdey
Over-and-Under, or as urbane, or as insane,
Except Volodymyr Zelensky,
The incredible president of Ukraine.
Moonlight is falling straight down on Manhattan.
The streets tonight so what
Are smooth as satin.
I like to there and touch it here.

I'm standing on the landing
Of the splendid Claridge's staircase.
I'm standing on the landing.
I look down at the lobby.
The marble shines like syrup.
So what they whip the marble with a riding crop
To keep the lava from Vesuvius away from us
And keep Pompeii plush and posh.

What's happening is a tragedy
Nonstop on our smart TV.
We look at it for hours and see
Tragedy and see
Nothing is more useless than poetry.
Tell the rabbi, confess it to your priest.
Poetry doesn't matter in the least.
Mariupol, Bucha, Odesa—Putin's nightmare feast.

London is melodious.
Mount Street Gardens is across the street so what
From Audley House where Purdey's is,
But atrocities in Ukraine are not far away,
And World War III not so far away.
Birdsong is serious.
Poetry is meaningless.
Poetry is a disgrace on a warm spring day in March.

You look at the sky with unconditional love.
What are the odds?
You count the clouds.
A man with a big plastic bag
Is kidnapping pigeons
In bunches off the streets of Manhattan
To sell to gun clubs in the suburbs
Where they will be released and shot for sport.

Tolstoy and Turgenev target
Hospitals and schools and Jews.
Pushkin and Pasternak and Babel light the fuse.
Tsvetaeva and Akhmatova don't refuse.
Mandelstam lights up the sky
Above his gulag with unconditional love
For long-range missiles. Tchaikovsky and Death
Want to defeat Ukraine.

Someone is being pushed off
The 96th Street subway platform onto the tracks and
The oncoming train screams. So what.
The problem of homelessness in the subways—
Having nowhere to undress—
Infests the downtown No. 3 Express.
You lift a hundred-thousand-dollar Purdey Trigger Plate
Over-and-Under wonder to your shoulder and levitate.

The gun goes *pop pop* so what
And the birds drop and you can't stop!
Just like that time on Ragged Island, off the coast of Maine,
Where pranksters had wickedly released a white rabbit pair
That proceeded to multiply and eat the innocent island bare.
You grabbed your gun for some grim fun
And a million rabbits—not knowing they were white—
Hid stock-still in plain sight.

So what.

HOW TO WRITE A POEM

I'm springing up and down for art
On a metaphorical swimming pool diving board,
Waving above my head the inhuman sword,
And other things you need to start.

I had a plan to race my motorcycle,
My racetrack-only Superbike racer,
Around Manhattan Island,
River to river,

At at least a hundred miles an hour,
At a very early morning hour to avoid traffic,
Down the FDR Drive to begin,
Up the West Side Highway to Spuyten Duyvil,

Having as a model the great French short film
C'était un rendez-vous of 1976 by Claude Lelouch,
Which ends up on top of Montmartre
After roaring through sleeping Paris.

My cancer is springing up and down
On a diving board above an empty pool,
No water in the pool, though it's August, it's summer,
So balance, yes balance, don't fall, make sense.

My cancer of the lung
Is springing up and down,
On a diving board
Above an empty pool,

No water in the pool,
Though it's August, it's summer,
So balance, yes balance,
Don't fall, make sense.

AT CHRISTMAS

I'd come back to the U.S.—Christmas 1955—
To Ezra Pound still in chains in Washington, D.C.,
At St. Elizabeths Hospital for the Criminally Insane
(*No apostrophe in St. Elizabeths*).
Why hadn't Archibald MacLeish got him out yet?
I was Rimbaud,
Not quite old enough by law to buy a drink in a bar,
But bulletproof and murderous,
With an air of debonair and assassination.
I was talkative and silent, up on the balls of my feet.

Days of snow padded the sparkling silence—still 1955—
Of my friend's Princeton dorm, empty at Christmas,
No one around, the sound of Bach from somewhere,
The smell of snow still falling, snow in my nostrils,
Snow outside the windows
My breath steamed up,
A foghorn of silence inflaming the air.
The father of the girl showed up with his two Great Danes
Just before dawn, when she had just gone,
To ask if his daughter was there.

People obsess when they can't move their bowels,
Which can go on for days.
Old people obsess especially.
People don't always talk about
What they obsess about—

Which leads to poetry.
People are flying through the tropical flowering trees
And playing musical instruments of joy.
Put your shotgun down and make peace.
This poem is for Mark Peploe who is dying.

Ghosts are
Having drinks in the loggia
At S. Francesco di Paola,
Still alive, years ago, looking forward
To what is now our past.
I can't tell you how many cigarettes we smoke.
If you climb to the top of the hilltop and look out,
Suddenly, like a moment in cinema,
The whole town is there and there's the Cathedral dome!
Clare and Bernardo and Mark and I are drinking wine.

THE PROBLEM WITH HAVING
A DOG

So here comes the argument
In favor of *not*,
In the form of this woman
Walking down the street

And into the hotdog place
At 72nd and Broadway
Right across from the subway's
72nd Street entrance to Lethe.

The woman is a ghost.
She died Wednesday.
Now she's eating a hotdog at the counter
With sauerkraut and mustard.

I've known her all my life.
She was the Radcliffe roommate of my former wife.
She married and divorced
My Harvard roommate.

I've often said the problem
With having a dog
Is that it's going to die before you do.
Almost certainly this is true.

That's why you might not want
To live alone
But on the other hand
You might not want a dog.

Jimmy, my dog, I don't miss you.
It's too painful to.
I can't remember you.
The ghost keeps eating, eating,

Standing right there transparently,
Across from the entrance to the subway,
At a counter of thin air,
And gulping down a papaya juice of nowhere.

LONG STORY SHORT

I'm not as old as I used to be.
I'm getting young.
I find myself making child nonsense sounds
Doing my exercises
When no one's around.
I find myself shouting at the floor.
I explode with rage and age.

My infancy is incomplete outside on the street
Pretending to be fleet
By how I look when I walk—which is acting—
Because in fact I am slow and ready to trip.
Underneath
I'm an old man full of baby.
You wouldn't know I'm a baby, maybe.

When my wife asks me why I'm looking so forlorn,
I curl my lip in baby scorn.
Women line up for me and lie down in love.
I'm an unlicensed doctor in a fake white coat
Delivering babies when I'm a baby
On my way to younger and younger
And the coffin of being unborn.

Oh, could I lose all death now!
Oh, if I could lose my death!
Farewell, thou child of my right hand and joy—

Me! Myself! And my many motorcycles of youth!
Look how the Mississippi River
Turns into a puddle of tears
In the coffin of being unborn!

ELLA SINGING A SONG

If I were the size of my thumbnail
Instead of the size of the room I'm in,
Or our house in Brooklyn I'm in,
Or the whole world outside,

And if I had a dog,
Which is what I want,
And could spend more time in Woodstock, Vermont,
I mean Woodstock, New York,

And see snakes and a bear,
And if life was fair,
I would be there
And swim all day long

With my mom and my dad and my granddad,
And they'd be glad,
And I'd be good,
And fly on the wings of a dragonfly over the pond.

MY ME

I'm not as old as I used to be,
I'm getting young.
I find myself making child nonsense sounds
Doing my exercises—
No one's around.
I find myself shouting on the floor.
I suddenly explode with rage and age.

My infancy is incomplete outside on the street
Pretending to be fleet
By how I look when I walk, which is acting,
Because in fact I am slow and ready to trip
And fall humiliatingly underneath
An old man full of baby.
You wouldn't know I'm a baby, maybe.

Women are waiting in the waiting room
When my wife asks me if they're still there.
I look through the keyhole
At blondes, brunettes, even the beautiful redhead
In that museum in France
Who fifty years ago went smiling into the sky,
And that girl from Texas who said I'll show

You mine if you show me yours, said the Texas girl.
Farewell, thou child of my right hand and joy—
My best piece of poetry—my me! Loved boy!
Look how the mighty Mississippi
Starts from a puddle at its source
And a mouthful of being unborn and turns into
St. Louis and myself!

SAG HARBOR

I have nothing to say
Which is an odd way
To begin, I suppose.

Having reached the point
At which there is
Almost no point.

Why not walk out
Into the water until
You can't.

It's just a little spot of black
On the back
Of your wrist.

Don't go on.
Don't go in.
Thunder and lightning.

We need the rain.
The crescent of the marina wants you
To walk a bit away

Before the storm starts
And wait it out
On the American Hotel porch

Eating the lovely club sandwich made with lobster
Which lets you forget America is over
After three centuries of four-leaf clover

And how red
The hotdogs sobbing
On the grill about to burst were.

Covid and clover!
Main Street to Glover,
America is over.

Firecrackers
Are going off
Despite the damp.

Porpoising in the pool
On this July Fourth holy day,
My naiad beauty Mitzi is swimming in the rain!

COME BACK, META BURDEN, DON'T BE DEAD

The computer keyboard is talking to the man.
The man needs a talking-to.
Talk, talk, talk.
Tap, tap, tap.
Each of them is about to take a nap.
Right there at the computer,
Sitting in his new desk chair,
The man is falling to his death thinking
About preposterously beautiful Meta Burden
Refusing to listen and skiing herself into an avalanche.
The man is imagining her last moments under the snow
And is falling asleep.
So that's what it's like?
Come back, Beauty, don't be dead.

WHITNEY ELLSWORTH

Whitney Ellsworth drives up in his early
1950s Citroën, the French black classic
You see in old French movies,
Super exotic in Cambridge, Massachusetts,
And says, "Want to go for a ride?" A blond boy.
The year is 1955 or 1954.
There is no Arthur Whitney Ellsworth no more.
He was the nicest human being my life has produced,
With a father, it appeared, as the source.
Kindly Duncan Ellsworth had a beautiful house
In Connecticut and another in Vermont and another on Fishers Island.
I have many memories of each place.

Do you want to take a ride? And I get in
And as we drive off, I wake from my dream.

CLAUDIO CASTIGLIONE

I was invited for a long weekend
To the house
On the Italian Riviera of Claudio Castiglione,
The Italian motorcycle magnate who owned MV Agusta
And Ducati and who of course knew
I was trying to get the Museum of Modern Art in New York
To display the melodious Ducati 916 as a work of art.

On our drive up from Bologna
In his comfortable businessman's Alfa,
I noticed we were calmly moving at almost
The speed of light on the autostrada
When a red Ferrari Testarossa exploded
Past us making the sound of God.
It turned out Claudio
Had a Testarossa
All his own at home.

How nice to be at his house and eat and talk
And walk with him and his gracious wife.
He told me of his plans to make
A garden with fruit trees and a house next door for his son.
He surprised me by asking me if I would
Like to accompany him on a visit to his late father's tomb.
It was clear the invitation meant a lot to him.

The next day,
Claudio and I visited the birthday cake of candles
For his Pharaoh and beloved founder
And beloved father and visited
The dead dad.

STEVE AARON

You were the loudest of us all by far,
And the sweetest behind your fear,
Brilliant expositor of Arthur Miller and Shakespeare.
There you are, at the beginning of your career,

Bellowing like a carny barker
In the Freshman Commons, selling tickets to some
HDC production with your tuba voice and bigger nose.
The stylish fellows like myself were appalled.

Steve Aaron was a lot brasher than was posh,
And a lot shyer, and smart.
Suddenly he was mounting a staging of Eliot's
Murder in the Cathedral to stop your head and start your heart.

The most gifted man in Harvard theater
In thirty years.
I remember him in Manhattan in analysis
Right across from the American

Museum of Natural History and its tattered old stuffed whale.
Aaron had an ungovernable phobic fear of the whale.
He asked me to go with him, literally holding hands,
So he could stare it down with an analytic harpoon—

And then backed out.
Years later, Goldie—his mother—pulled out of a closet
A brush-and-mirror set meant for a baby,
For baby Steve, and scrimshawed into the ivory back

Of each item was a tiny spouting whale!
The psychoanalyst's name was Tannenbaum.
One day, Aaron came in and, after lying down, said: "I don't know why—
There's this tune I can't get out of my head! Tum *Tum* tee tum. Tum *Tum* tee tum.

'O Christmas tree! O Christmas tree!'" Steve,
You're a blue forest of oceans, seagulls flying their cries.
I come from an unimaginably different plan.
I've traveled to you because my technology can.

I ride the cosmos on my poetry Ducati, Big Bang engine, einsteinium forks.
Let me tell you about the extraterrestrial Beijings and New Yorks.
You are the planet Earth, where my light-beam spaceship will land.
I'll land after light-years of hovering and take your hand.

JAR

Geniuses like us with private parts
Approach each other in fits and starts,
Reproach each other and coach each other
And fall in love
And then Oh brother!—
We're afraid we'll smother.

All us big beating hearts,
Circle around
With our big beating parts,
And our Harvard smarts—
But without a white bright shore
What's it for?

The jeweler's name is JAR,
For Joel Arthur Rosenthal,
Where genius blends a swan with a giraffe,
Combining kinds of gracefulness,
In Place Vendôme, in Paris!
Joel made a genius wristwatch,

Made the thing in platinum,
Shaped it like a skipping stone.
Joel visited an old friend
In Wainscott, out East, on Long Island,
And left behind my genius watch:
New strap, new life,

New strap, new life,
My genius watch,
Cleaned, restored, refreshed.
It's nice to have you here, dear.
Millions every day die
With no one dear near.

RIMBAUD AND VERLAINE

People with private parts
Approach each other in fits and starts.
Get it wrong, it briefly hurts,
But after one more loop de loop it squirts
Enough to lubricate the whole outdoors
And then you go inside to wax the floors.
Verlaine is whining.
Rimbaud is like a swimming pool of sunlight shining.
And now the sun sheds its outer lining
And the two men rob
Each other homicidally and turn the doorknob.
The world is entirely doorknob—
But without a door—
But what in the world for?

TO BAUDELAIRE

In the full-length mirror all the glass is you.
I do
What women tell me to.
I look between her legs and see a Subaru
Parking on Fifth Avenue.
And there's an owl who hoots *who who*
And has a dirty mind like me and hoots *who who*.
In French the *louve* adores the rascal *loup*—
The two go at it like a toothy glue.
Her eyes go *baaa*. His go *mooo*.
Her thighs go *cock-a-doodle-do*.
Garter belt and stockings strutting down Fifth Avenue
In high heels and nothing else shout *Who!* who, *Who!* who.
Garter belt and stockings strutting down Fifth Avenue
With attitude shout *One!* two, *One!* two.
I'm happy when I see her Subaru
When she bends down to touch her toes and kiss her shoe.
Figaro! Figaro! Figaro! Subaru! Subaru! Subaru!
Subah-ru!
Louve and Loup
Go at it like goats or gods or gobs of goo
In Room 1002 (ten oh two),
Room with a view, Central Park, too.
Black straps of the garter belt zap the zoo
Between her stockings into honeydew.
You see the Subaru
Parking on Fifth Avenue.

You see a Subaru
Parking in the mirror under skies of blue
When she bends down to touch her toes for you
Because she wants you to enjoy the view
Of her woke flower singing teardrops of dew
Which reheating makes only better, like a stew!
Petals and stamen, clitoris, Muslim, Christian, Hindu, Jew.
It's true
A few
NATO leaders are women, true—
A few.

ST. LOUIS BLUES

The man who dropped two atom bombs on
London
Was Harry Truman
From Missouri.
I know a woman with a rescue dog named Truman.
I'd like to mix in nonsense
While there's time left
Before it ends.
My sister was too young to walk, I think.
I'm standing by the radio
And waiting for the asteroid.
I think of you.

I'm waiting in St. Louis for my sister,
Five million years younger than I am, to catch up.
I'm looking out the window.
Why was I born? Why am I living?
Is playing on the radio, Jerome Kern's corny song,
And I am singing along.
I think I was a pigeon
With a strong sense of mission
That got me to my ledge
Among the pigeons in New York,
A lifetime later,
Moaning and mating.

A pigeon walks into my New York study
Through a slightly open window
And can't figure out, no more than I can,
How to get back out.
The window was cracked open to relieve
The heat.
In the weird millions of years before the dinosaurs,
In the darkness of the dark wood of the Oxford Apartments,
In the unbreathable burning air,
And already pretending I wasn't a Jew,
I waited for the enormous
And the asteroid.

Little atoms are bubbling
From the boiling surface
Millions of years before
The dinosaurs appear.
I am waiting
In St. Louis.
In St. Louis, the sky is burping and the oceans
Heave convulsively
And a sweat of ammonia
In the little marble lobby
And up the marble stairs
Is my beginning.

An ecstasy of nothingness
Is the known universe.
The dinosaurs on planet Earth
Will be extinguished.
I knew a woman with a rescue dog named Truman
Who knew something new was coming
And parked her car in Forest Park.
Soon of course it would be dark.
On all sides was the winged wonder
Of giant prehistoric thunder
And lovely long-necked dinosaurs with tiny eyes,
Making tiny frightened cries.

1937

It's always about to rain except
When it's already raining, like now.
They go from the pub to the cinema through the rain,
To the newsreel and the Disney cartoon,
With tickets that are half-price

One day a week in the afternoon.
It was the Basque city of Guernica last week,
Weeping under airplanes dropping bombs.
Walt Disney is not Picasso,
But his art is gloriously sunny,

But Mickey Mouse has already said
The poems of Lorca will never be funny.
Disney, the century's genius, makes amends.
Only he can make butterflies
And hurricanes make friends.

D. H. Lawrence is a kamikaze
Burning up the sky
On his way to bite
England explosively and die.
He has bad English teeth

That are sharp as a shark
And a burning brain
That sings like a lark.
Silkworms eat mulberry leaves to feed
Rainer Maria Rilke the silk he needs

To address the angelic orders.
Even the enormous angels
Dismount from the sublime, dismount
From Pegasus, the horse with wings,
And instead of wine, sip brine.

The nostrils of the T. S. Eliot crocodile
Lurk just above the surface of the river Nile.
His periscope is two nostrils that watch like eyes.
His snout stays submerged
In water bitter as bile.

Kisses of passion grunt like electroshock
And cause convulsions and rigor mortis
And sexually join together
Two hard-shelled hunchbacks,
Each shaped like a tortoise.

They're Eliot, they're Lawrence,
Each honking on and on, on his moral high horse.
If Lawrence caught her,
Lawrence would slaughter
Emily Dickinson, Eliot's daughter.

Some will get sick and some will die
But that is not the reason why
A small plane
Tows an advertisement
For a nearby bar and restaurant

Through the sky
Above the beach at Gibson Lane.
It is the opposite of insane.
Everybody knows Pete the pilot.
It's his plane,

Which he crashes without harm now and again.
Black marvelous waves, white August,
Is the summer song of Gibson Beach.
There's a skywriting plane crossing the sun
With a marriage proposal from someone for someone.

STALIN

There's a book I have called *Shotgun Shooting*.
I got it from my son.
Put the muzzle in your mouth.
Careful with your teeth.
Pull the trigger with your toe.
Think of someone dead who desperately feared death.
Susan Sontag? Philip Larkin? God bless everyone!
I don't believe in God. I believe in fun.

Stalin telephones Boris Pasternak
From the Kremlin to tell him Mandelstam,
Who has been arrested, will be all right,
And is a bit surprised when
Pasternak does not particularly react.
Stalin hangs up.
He is Stalin.
All this is not far from St. Louis.

The treasurer of my father's company
Was a saintly man named David Stein
Whose wet lyrical eyes
Had the sweetness of a sound.
Stein lived for music
But didn't play an instrument
But knew personally every distinguished
Musician in those war years.

My father and my uncle—
The bosses in their office—
Looked up from their twin desks
At each other or out the window
At miles of piles of coal under snow
At the Seidel Coal and Coke Company on Vandeventer,
Bituminous and anthracite
Blackly under white.

Blue trucks are waiting,
One an old rhinoceros
With an outside drive chain on a sprocket
Like a bicycle.
We deliver heat.
We give heat to the cold.
We give heat to the young and the old
And even to the poor who can't pay.

A GIRAFFE EATING A SWAN

When I get to heaven
The thing I know I'll hear
Is the hissing of the trees
On a heavenly day in Central Park,
Trees in a breeze seen from above
On fire with green fireworks
Of sunlight messing with their hair.

When I'm up there in heaven looking down
I'll see the treetops of the trees
Writhing like spaghetti on the boil
And Central Park praying on its knees
To me up here.
Old age turns me into a lobster in boiling water
Screaming for help silently.

On the East Side, down one-way Fifth Avenue,
On the West Side, up Central Park West,
The police cars warble
And the fire engines toot.
A swan is eating a giraffe
And the other way around.
It's the New York sound.

Since when did anyone ask the lobster
How it felt about the water getting warmer?
The warming water is supposed to numb the lobster.

Not that I notice.
My dark shell will turn red
When I'm edibly dead.
That's not what anyone said.

Police are pouring down Fifth Avenue.
A man apparently has stabbed
To death a young Hasidic Jew
Outside the entrance to the zoo.
Local news programs are there now, too—
Already repeating endlessly this new
Central Park news that it turns out isn't true.

O city infested with scaffolding
That never comes down
And botches the buildings it's meant to save!
O covered pedestrian passageways that remind me
Of my beloved Bologna and its *portici*!
I lived five quarters of my life
Riding my Ducati race bikes near death there.

At night I regret
This and that I did or didn't in my life
But it doesn't blight delight the way
Arthritis does.
I used to ride my motorcycles
On top of witty, pretty girls.
I still stalk sex at eighty-six.

PANDEMIC SPRING

Hardhats wearing hard hats build the building going up—
Nineteen floors so far—one noisy Broadway block away.
Sometimes the construction site hollers
And howls like the ocean
From the pain of turning into apartments.
Saws rip the morning open
Promptly at seven.

They're dressed in yellow to be more visible
In case they fall off into the roaring—
Wriggling specks of yellow rice
In safety harnesses they attach to God.
Up and down, right and left, back and forth
Is the story of your life until you're
Floating in outer space where of course

There is no up and down
Or wet rain turning into summer.
This poem is the wah-wah mute in my trumpet—
Otherwise, I'd scream.
Up and down, back and forth, the rocking motion
Of someone walking down the street
While the building goes on going up, now twenty floors.

A camel with a single hump,
Long eyelashes and soft big eyes,
Is my late father, a hunchback and gentleman.

Nothing. Nothing.
Nothing.
No one. No one.
No one.

Meanwhile, a flesh-eating angel,
The size of Tyrannosaurus rex,
But with wings of gold and claws of crystal
And fish scales for skin, oh so slowly
Flies with profoundly vast wingbeats OF THUNDER
Invisibly up and down the avenue in silence,
Singing hallelujah.

MOXIFLOXACIN

I know down from up and this ain't up.
The street flows like an ice floe down the street.
Buildings on either side bow from the waist mockingly,
Mocking me.
A center strip of green, which
For some reason they call a mall, divides
Uptown and downtown traffic from each other,
Going north and going south from each other.
I'm talking to the sky, which doesn't hear me of course
Because of the traffic noise or whatever.

Never mind the ice floe.
I'm thinking about how hot it is.
I'm thinking about the wonderful Laure de Gourcuff,
Whom many years ago I was almost in love with,
Pronounced *de Goorkoof*.
I want to say something extreme.
She was as quiet as a leaf.
I want to say something intense.
How peculiar to have pneumonia in this heat,
Which I've just learned I have.

A patch one-inch-square that the CT scan
Detected inspires
The use of antibiotic megatonnage
To wipe the inflammation off the face of the earth.

You're printed on my lung, darling, and on my mind.
I am getting young.
So many years have passed.
It's as if I were making it up.
There we were, down in the Cher,
At their ugly château the size of an apartment building.

Oh, my pneumonia!
You and I are about to take a big plane to England.
Do I need permission from my moxifloxacin?
I just said to my girlfriend,
Whom I will see in London, I said,
Is that a nice way to talk
On Father's Day to New York?
To the four wheels of your car,
The steering wheel of your life,
The horn that honks you?

CAPE COAST SLAVE CASTLE, GHANA

Main Street flows like the Mississippi
Under my study window
And carries the N-word away downstream.
The old distinguished Black community in Sag Harbor,

Civilized, sophisticated,
Counts on a comfortable cabin
On a cruise ship to somewhere nice,
Despite the coronavirus threat and the heat.

Way down upon the Swanee River,
Far, far away.
That's where my heart is yearning ever,
Now that I have air-conditioning in my study.

Now that I have air-conditioning in my study,
I know that I will live forever.
You see me at my desk, whitely
Writing what you're reading.

The Negro chauffeur
Hosed the soap off
The whitewall tires he had just scrubbed clean.
He polished the big black car

And cried
Because Franklin Delano Roosevelt had just died.
I was a little white boy
And the chauffeur was my friend.

African Americans come thousands of miles
To pose for photographs
In front of the blindingly white buildings
Of Cape Coast Castle in the African sun,

And walk beneath their feet on a pilgrimage
To the castle's underground dungeon
That holds their shackled ancestors
In the millions of darkness,

So the two sides can trade places
And one can be the other,
And travel back and travel forward
From horror to Sag Harbor.

SONG

I licked the sidewalk.
I ate the air.
I did anything and went anywhere.
I had wings and could hold my breath forever.
I walked on water—but everybody walks on water.
I talked nonstop underwater.
I warbled underwater, cooing like a dove.
I got into my Gulfstream jet and flew high above
But also flew low below.
Then I turned thirteen and wrote a poem.
The sea pours in while my heart pours out.
At thirteen, I wrote you a letter from Sarasota, Florida.
Then I turned eighty-three.
The third half of my life begins.

PARKINSON'S

The instructor expects you to respect
Every bolt pimpling the skin
Of the little airplane
Before you climb in

For your first lesson.
Also, John Wilkes Booth
Wants to meet
President Lincoln.

It's as if no one even noticed
A man on water skis in the downtown traffic,
Going a bit fast actually,
Behind smiling dolphins.

I'm waterskiing on asphalt.
I'm making an airplane sound.
Two dolphins tow me on my skis down Broadway.
There's plenty of traffic. No one stares. No one cares.

You think you're seeing things.
You see a man with wings.
He lifts off into the sky
Above Columbus Circle.

My eyes are bluer than the sky is.
I don't want to be POTUS.
President of the United States.
Don't tell me *united*.

Walt Whitman and Ulysses Grant
Merge at dawn
To bake
Fresh American daylight.

MARCH

God made human beings so dogs would have companions.
Along the promenade dogs are walking women.
One is wearing fur
Although the day is warm.

The fur
Trots behind a cur.
The mongrel sparkles and smiles
Leading her by the leash.

The month of March, that leads to hell,
Is plentiful in Cap Ferrat.
There is gambling around the bend
In the bay at the Casino in creamy Monte Carlo.

White as the Taj Mahal,
White as that stove of grief,
Is the cloud.
Just passing by.

The air is herbs.
The sea is blue chrome curls.
The mutt sparkles and leers
And lifts a leg.

White as the weightless Taj Mahal,
White as the grief and love it was,
The day is warm, the sea is blue.
The dog, part spitz, part spots, is zest

And piss and Groucho Marx
Dragging a lady along.
The comedy
Is raw orison.

Dogs need an owner to belong to.
Dogs almost always die before their owners do.
But one dog built a Taj Mahal for two.
I loved you.

ROYA

Meet beautiful Roya Shanks
And what a beautiful name she has
Who presides over the restaurant Odeon
And what a beautiful job she does.

Meet marvelous, gorgeous Roya Shanks,
A hostess of magnificent and friendly hauteur
Who dresses in a way all her own
In dresses that are unique and colorful and stunning.

Picture the universe that surrounds
Odeon and this beautiful woman,
This wonderful woman with a wonderful name.
The universe is in the small and in the largest.

And then there is the man
Who dropped dead on his birthday.
He couldn't believe it. Too good to be true.
With his new book of poems about to be out.

But then on the other hand
There's Frank O'Hara walking along the beach
Run over by a beach taxi on Fire Island in 1966.
He died with as they say everything to live for.

Frank was probably drunk and it was late
But what a silly fate. How stupid.
Aroused like Venus being pissed on by Cupid.
Dead three days later.

Life isn't an elevator in the lobby
Waiting to whisk you up to the spiritual
But beautiful Roya Shanks
Seats you in your favorite booth.

SUMMERTIME

A zigzag of lightning,
No bigger than a butterfly, flutters
Across the room into my eyes,
Your razor laser that can blind.

You do that, what you're doing,
Which chokes the windpipe
But lets the lovely rain in.
Here comes the rain!

How sweet the smell is.
Rain on cement!
Hot suddenly not.
The dog has to go out.

The baby has to be changed.
The baby has to be fed.
Here comes the rain.
The dog has to go out.

There's a drought.
It's raining too hard for the rain to help.
With one big gulp,
The ground will drown.

BUBBLES

Bubbles
Are floating up
From something that has sunk.
You've never seen the sky above so blue.
But there is nothing you can do.

A dead horse lying in the street
Either means it's Central Park South
And a carriage horse
From a horse and carriage ride that's dropped dead
Or means it's 1914 just before the Great War.

A LITTLE DRINKING SONG BY DU FU

The ship of state has split in half
The cargo has spilled out
Dogs and cats and you and me
Have spilled into the deep blue sea

Have spilled into the bountiful
The beautiful the CGI
Rough seas getting rougher
Huge waves of red America the blue boats can't live through

And blue go down and blue go drown
And drink democracy and eat it all
And lick the dish
And taste a stinking prehistoric fish they've just eaten

How much they miss
How much they wish

NICK CAVE

Because the motorcycle is very light
Ducati called it the Superleggera
And very good-looking and vastly fast and made of light
And the factory would make only five hundred of them

And stop. Which would make it rare.
And one was lucky to have one for sixty-five thousand dollars
And that was quite some years ago and a lot of money.
Mine poses on its stand expensively unridden right there.

And the enormous beauty of the poet and singer Nick Cave
Issuing his impossibly lyrical notice of unending grief
Over the son he has lost and the love and the life.

And the superlight lifting into the light. And only art can.
I have written this poem for you, Nick,
This awkwardly unrhymed sonnet meant to not make sense.

YOU'VE COME A LONG WAY
FROM ST. LOUIS

When Uncle Art took me up in his plane
He forgot to tell me not to stick out my hand.
I was violently blown backwards
Into poetry, high
In the sky above Missouri,
Above banjo-strumming river towns sipping the Mississippi.
I was aloft and reborn, a brief rebirth,
But then the engine
Snored us back down to earth.

In the days of my youth,
When I was young,
We lived in the Senate Apartments
Next door to the Congress Hotel
On patriotically named Union Boulevard
That honored the Civil War.
My friend Henry Pflager and I, all of five years old,
Pretended to be in labor on the living room floor
The afternoon my sister was born.

In the days of my youth,
In those Seidel Coal and Coke Company days,
How green St. Louis was
And how clean St. Louis was.
Elegantly plain white lettering on the trucks
Delivered SEIDEL to the factories that brewed the famous beer.

From my bed in New York, I hear Forest Park's
Sweet summertime humidity that smells so sweet!
A million dream crickets hiss like a garden hose.

The company kept a box at Sportsman's Park
Between home plate and first.
I've seen the town and country cars that were
Parked out in front of our fancy address.
A man in our building
Limped miserably and was bitter
Because the surgeon had operated
Of course on the wrong leg
And made that leg shorter.

AUGUST ON SHELTER ISLAND

A housefly doesn't want to die
Any more than you or I.
Its tiny horsepower is of brief duration
Like treaties with the Choctaw Nation.
To flies, flyswatters are the atom bomb.
My poems are a Peeping Tom
Invading through a nighttime window
People doing what they want to do.

We come from America, the wack job.
We come to Afghanistan with names like Bob.
Flyswatters are the wrath and rod
Of the Almighty handheld God
Whose drone strikes catch houseflies
Flirting on the kitchen table
And smush their sexual filth to rubble.
A fly is what men's pants have in front, in English.

Once upon a time, Manhattan was sweet.
Elegant Rizzoli's Bookstore sold
Luxury art books on a fancy street
Alongside albums of beautiful motorcycles
And African crocodiles in superb photographs
Masturbating for the well-heeled effete elite
In the days before women finally had the whip hand
In a changed (or anyway changing) land.

The girls and women of Afghanistan
Devour the dreaded, bearded penises of the Taliban
In the traditional Afghan dish of Eat the Man
Which is prepared in various ways
In various recipes
To punish those according to their iniquities.
Tal Tal Taliban
Kill the Tal but eat the man.

There's typically no plumbing in an outhouse—
Your hole sits on the hole.
Out comes Shelter Island, Long Island—
The size of a tadpole.
The Muse squatted over a stand-up toilet in Paris,
Her hole aiming for the hole.
Of course, the way things are going,
The planet has already ended.

Diarrhea and constipation—precious pair of poets—
Sing their stanzas tunelessly.
No music is the Muse. The Muse is a hole.
The Muse could barely breathe last Saturday.
Try thinking of something nicer to say than COPD,
Perhaps something not about sex.
Try thinking something else above the waist.
Climb up the moonlight to the moon.

That gorgeous, enormous Japanese cherry tree outside
Holds the record for being, at least in America, the biggest.
America is big on big and likes records.

The tree is rare—and stupendous.
You have never been enclosed by such love
As in this garden that makes you feel at once
Captured and released,
As if you were in the arms of a beautiful breast.

It's a fighter jet's midair refueling by its airborne wet nurse
Taking place at five thousand feet,
Looking down at whitecaps
Crashing on the green palm-fringed beach
Where Polynesian human sacrifice still takes place.
The Muse refuels the poet through a midair refueling hose
Stiffly stretching down from her big Muse nose.
And sunlight pours down through the rainbow.

Trees are dancing with trees
Like a corps de ballet
Flinging themselves desperately this way and that way
In a modern-dance-y manner in the blasts of wind.
The trees shake their costumes and sort of settle.
I can't get your body out of my head
Now that your body has fled. The wind dies down.
The love and the loss continue, of course.

White butterflies
Flutter over the silent swimming pool,
A pool of silent blue.
Confetti of white butterflies pixelate the view.

Empty deck chairs return to the lawn after the storm.
Each emptiness stands for someone trying to breathe.
So many died but kept on living anyway
On local oysters from Peconic Bay.

It's Shelter Island—love song and retort—
Between Sag Harbor and Greenport.
I have just spoken to my old friend Mr. Ezra Pound,
Whose girlfriend handed him her cellphone
In a car driving them through Berlin.
What a wondrous world, before we died, we were in,
Speaking from Shelter Island Heights Pharmacy
To E.P. in Berlin.

I love you so much I could eat you alive.
The chartered jet flies into my mouth
With the Muse in it,
Headed for East Hampton Airport,
Call letters HTO. She steps out.
"Get thee behind me, Satan—and PUSH!"
She wants me to enter her tush?
I want to!

She doesn't want any such thing!
She wants the freedom to be and sing.
She wants to be able to pry off the big babies who cling.
She wants to outdo, outsell, outlast, outblast

All the competitors, perhaps
Especially Penguin Random House.
I saw her an hour ago swimming off Wades Beach,
Zigzags of lightning in her hair.

WHAT THOU LOVEST WELL
REMAINS

The most beautiful woman who ever was
Is what the crematorium does.
The crematorium oven is the last one
Who gets to be with everything she is:
Wit, heart, lungs, voice, beauty, brain, in an urn
They present you with for sprinkling the ashes around.
It is a fearful thing to love what death can touch.

So I take the elevator down
Instead of the staircase now.
No flying down the stairs, no more.
How rare to—
Once in a lifetime—
Meet someone who
Makes you stop and stare forever.

I'm sitting in a chair at a desk.
I'm walking down a street.
It's hot summer. It's cold winter. It's not nowhere.
I was a comer
Once. I walked around in a mummy case of glamour.
I coulda been a contender
Is the line I remember,

Instead of a bum, which is what I am.
Underneath the Harvard hoodie, it was me.
Tap tap tap tap . . . that's the computer keyboard,
Not the sound of a white cane and impaired sight.
I wake from a dream in which the three blond siblings
Who occupy the tall house in Belgravia's Chapel Street,
Two girls and a boy, eternal, immortals,

Are all still here
In their dazzling twenties, happily orphaned, that is to say
Both parents alive but keeping out of the way,
No parent around, a dream.
Getting up in the middle of the night
Is what you have to do sometimes if you write—
And you turn on the light.

SONNET

I'm talking to my body—I say
I know you can't live without me.
And I know
You'll one day go away.
I was talking to my body
The other day.
I knew what to say.
I said *Don't go. Stay.*
How much do I weigh?
Not much. Less and less.
Especially in the face.
Tumbleweed fills the New York Public Library
Main reading room on Forty-Second Street
With tumbleweed.

ONE AFTERNOON

You see your mother napping
Naked on her afternoon bed
And you freeze
Because her legs are spread

And you stay,
Standing in the hallway, outside a doorway,
Your whole life long,
Long after you can't.

What a chance to see
A woman completely.
That it was
Your mother was

White as bread, with writing on it,
Writing a sonnet.

ROBERT KENNEDY AND
LYNDON JOHNSON

I. LYNDON

I wish I was an empty lot
With just a toilet and a cot.
Except I sometimes wish I'd been in politics.
Except they're all a bunch of pricks.
The four racing motorcycles I own snore
On their stands on a Dallas showroom floor.
My Ducati Desmosedici, my Ducati Supermono,
My Superleggera, my 999, roar no more.
Alas, I have to sell them because I have to
Give up going vastly fast because I'm eighty-four.
Every morning when I shave
Is one day closer to the grave.

I lather ever closer to extinction, I rave over my grave.
What you and I don't give the nation, Robert Kennedy gave.
What used to be a soaring American river
Is now a trickle from a shiver.
Fearless Bobby Kennedy was killed.
It was as unlikely as blue sky over London—
Assassination being so American—
That his precious life would not be spilled.
Too much napalm and too much LSD
Leads us straight to LBJ

Dropping his trousers outdoors to shit
In front of a cabinet officer visiting his ranch.

That's how crude the great Lyndon Johnson could be,
Who did more for the poor than anyone since FDR,
Once Lee Harvey Oswald had assassinated JFK.
We need you back, Barack, God knows.
The prep for a colonoscopy,
The emptying out that leaves the colon clean and free,
Is what the nation needs so it can clearly see
The malignant Trump presidency.
How many years before the Trump malignancy
Untreated means the United States will die?
What's the life expectancy, how long can we live with this lout?
Well, as Philip Larkin said, in another connection, we shall find out.

2. VIETNAM

I stood on the top step outside St. Patrick's
After attending the funeral service.
I was the first to leave the cathedral and the day was empty,
With thousands of silent mourners in the silent street.
I stood alone for a long minute staring out at Fifth Avenue.
Then the doors behind me opened and out poured the silent crowd.
Teddy Kennedy
Had broken down eulogizing his brother.
Robert Kennedy, the senator from New York,
Was also a candidate for president
Who had just won the California Democratic primary
When he was shot and killed, killed and shot. Oh no.

The space at the bottom of the stairs
Was roped off by the police.
No one down there was allowed to get too near.
The space at the bottom of the stairs was silence.
I don't forget the famous incident
When the president of the United States, in his cowboy boots,
Squatted in a field to empty his bowels
In front of a cabinet officer he was showing around his ranch.
Lyndon,
Who did more for Black people than anyone since Lincoln,
Isn't Trump
But liked to have people around him when he took a dump.

I stand on the top step of the war in Vietnam,
Looking out over the great grieving silence.
Those of us invited are supposed to board a special train
Waiting to take us to Washington for the burial at Arlington.
Right away, Ford pardoned Nixon
But the Nixon poison wasn't gone
Until one year later
With the fall of Saigon.
Ford pardons Nixon
But the Nixon poison isn't gone
Even one year later
With the fall of Saigon.

FRANK CONROY

I lived on hotdogs as a boy,
The only thing I'd eat.
My all-American food phobia
Lasted till I got over it
When I was thirty-five or thirty-six.
I had a passion for my car.
Oh, did I ever love flying around in that crazy Jaguar.
I was a jazz pianist with a long handsome face keeping the beat.
I was a creature from the bottom of the ocean, a jawbone with thick lips,
Which you can see in the painting used on the cover
Of *Stop-Time*, my marvelous book.
I was the head of the Iowa Writers' Workshop
When I got the news I was going to die.
I told the final specialist I hoped it wouldn't hurt.

A MATCHED PAIR OF PURDEYS

Seidel is a poet who likes politics
But has other topics.
Yeats announces to the crowd
That he expects the struggle to be garrulous, lavish,
Outrageous, Irish, glorious.

Bursts of pneumatic drilling in the street below
Shatter seven in the morning six floors above.
Verizon, the phone company,
Makes screams of annihilation
Connect the city.

The chic, berserk,
Museum-of-Modern-Art-New-York
Pneumatic drilling in my work
Is snow falling in the tropics
Noisily.

I syng of a mayden that is makeles.
I sing of a shotgun that is matchless.
A matched pair of Purdeys
Is a bespoke work of art
In Purdey's London gun room on South Audley Street.

Men wrote about beautiful women
In those days.
Yeats himself is guilty
Of too much beautiful-woman praise.
Women don't want that and will tear your tongue out

To make you politically correct.
It's a new generation
Of girls who generate Soviet-style show trials
To condemn
The pathetic older power generation of White Man.

It's a new generation
Of girls who generate Soviet-style
Show trials just
To condemn.
Ah men. Amen.

Yeats warns the shouting crowd
But don't become a mob!
One woman starts to sob.
Two weeks from now,
The woman will be shot dead.

This could only happen in the Kremlin.
This is Ireland.
The woman is a diamond.
Her father turns her in,
Then tries in vain to save her skin.

Down country lanes, on pitch-black nights,
The stars above switch on their brights,
No interference from city lights or human rights.
There's the Stalin constellation, there's Orion
In the arms of Hitler.

Yeats warns the government boys in Dublin
That Irish aristocrats and patriots fart
Green like Irish cattle fart
And then the poets
And the politicians start.

Local politicians fart
Bullshit from the heart.
That's the nature of their art,
Skywriting on the sky
Smoke that blows away.

It's always about to rain except
When it's already raining, like now.
They go from the pub to the cinema through the rain,
To the newsreel and the Disney cartoon,
With tickets that are half-price

One day a week in the afternoon.
It was the Basque city of Guernica last week,
Weeping under airplanes dropping bombs.
Walt Disney is not Picasso,
But his art is gloriously sunny,

But Mickey Mouse has already said
The poems of Lorca will never be funny.
Disney, the century's genius, makes amends.
Only he can make butterflies
And hurricanes make friends.

D. H. Lawrence is a kamikaze
Burning up the sky
On his way to bite
England explosively and die.
He has bad English teeth

That are sharp as a shark
And a burning brain
That sings like a lark.
Silkworms eat mulberry leaves to feed
Rainer Maria Rilke the silk he needs

To address the angelic orders.
Even the enormous angels
Dismount from the sublime, dismount
From Pegasus, the horse with wings,
And instead of wine, sip brine.

The nostrils of the T. S. Eliot crocodile
Lurk just above the surface of the river Nile.
His periscope is two nostrils that watch like eyes.
His snout stays submerged
In water bitter as bile.

Kisses of passion grunt like electroshock
And cause convulsions and rigor mortis
And sexually join together
Two hard-shelled hunchbacks,
Each shaped like a tortoise.

They're Eliot, they're Lawrence,
Each honking on and on, on his moral high horse.
If Lawrence caught her,
Lawrence would slaughter
Emily Dickinson, Eliot's daughter.

It ends in twenty twenty-two
Because a coup
Because of you
Because the midterm elections.
The United States will come apart in sections.

What started in the nest
Will break off first
But Florida is the worst,
Which coincides with launches into space
And global warming melting the Antarctic ice.

The best
Will break off first.
The planet
Starts to leak
Mountains with no peak. Don't look.

The pulse oximeter says
Love is not in human blood.
Your blood is mud.
Your blood is a red thud.
The pulse oximeter lies—

Love is!
All people talk about is Covid.
They don't talk about Virgil and Ovid.
In the Year of the Pandemic
Sources talk about how

Republicans are sick with longing
To serve the crown sitting on the severed head,
Removed for safety from the previous president.
Each president is previous to the next
In what was once.

Some will get sick and some will die
But that is not the reason why
A small plane
Tows an advertisement
For a nearby bar and restaurant

Through the sky
Above the beach at Gibson Lane.
It is the opposite of insane.
Everybody knows Peter Green.
It's his plane,

Which he crashes without harm now and again.
Black marvelous waves, white August,
And the summer song of Gibson Beach.
There's a skywriting plane crossing the sun
With a marriage proposal from someone for someone.

GENTLEMEN'S FINAL

I ought to be able to remember who I am
Because I am probably the king of Siam.
Or else I'm the royal elephant
The king has honored with a royal patent
To do the impossible
And cross the tropical Alps with a tropical Hannibal.

I'm the Gentlemen's Final at Wimbledon.
There are no gentlemen, but I am one.
I was the moon—now I'm the sun.
I'm the Gentlemen's Final at Wimbledon.
The pandemic has kidnapped my brains away.
The final takes place on Centre Court today.

The U.K. is fourteen lines long, which makes it a sonnet.
But don't bet your Brexit on it.

A FRESH START

What's a woman worth? What's a man?
What's a live-in maid who works for them?
But no one has a housemaid living in the house
These days, outside perhaps Afghanistan.

People don't have live-in maids living
In their apartments anymore.
They use the maid's former place
For storing pots and cookbooks and storage space.

The maid's room behind the kitchen will be
Re-plastered and repainted and turned
Into a pantry fitted out with shelves and hooks
To suit the new life and the hungry cookbooks.

Repainting is the point.
Repaint your life.
Repaint your husband and your wife.
Upgrade your empire to brighter.

It's like waiting at a stoplight for the light to change.
You're waiting for the red to turn to green.
Make yourself less stingy, less lean.
Make yourself happier by being a bit dirtier and less clean—

And paint it! And when you see the sky at last getting lighter
After a sleepless night waiting and waiting for dawn,
But you weren't willing to turn your light on,
And there's no sunrise between her thighs,

Or for that matter inside her also open eyes,
So that no matter how hard a person tries,
There's nothing but a brown cockroach
That makes a funny sound when it speaks.

MALKOVICH RECITES SENECA'S
THYESTES

It's a symphony orchestra
Of the House
And Senate in joint session
To hear the State of the Union.
Madam Speaker, the president of the United States!

And all of them are masturbating, beating their meat,
Frantically bowing their violins—about to come.
Here comes the president.
It's the republic reduced to the pubic.
E pubic unum! No wonder they get nothing done.

Now, a beautiful woman masturbating is a beautiful thing to see.
A beautiful woman masturbating is a beautiful thing to *be*.
Who said that? Stalin did, who also said
The death of one man is a tragedy.
The death of millions is a statistic.

I call the rubber sex doll that I live with Lydia.
I wake up every morning next to my Venus, Lydia.
Sometimes I don't know who we are or why.
I'm terrified to find out who—
This year, because of Covid, it will be by absentee ballot.

Last year when I was eighty-four,
And therefore not yet eighty-five,
I knew at least that I was still alive,
Which I don't know one year later
When I go to bed apparently to snore.

It's been said that so few peepholes actually exist
That no one knows exactly what's up.
I think of you walking on the moon,
And therefore upside down,
So I can see from underneath right up your dress.

Makes no sense.
I'm dreaming again
That I'm awake recounting the vote
So I can see from underneath Michigan,
Georgia, Wisconsin, Pennsylvania, Arizona.

The emperor Nero is playing golf in West Palm Beach.
The small ball is the world.
Migratory geese no longer travel south.
How can they if they don't?
They used to block the sky and foul the fields.

He plays badly and complains he actually won.
He orders his beloved tutor and mentor, Seneca,
To kill himself.
Everybody appreciates how great a man the golfer is.
That must be why they all applaud.

The dishwasher in the kitchen going through its cycle
Sounds uncannily like a foghorn in thick fog.
I think of Ragged Island
In insane
Thick fog off the coast of Maine.

Lydia, oh Lydia,
You gave me your love and your chlamydia,
But I couldn't get rid o' ya
Because of the heat in my heart
When my part entered your part and life turned into art.

And life turned into art,
And it was spring when it was autumn,
And the sweet was tart
Heat in my heart,
And my heart started to start.

Art is my scaffold, art is my noose
That I put around my neck myself
Standing on the trap.
Do you take this noose, for better for worse,
In sickness and in health, during Covid-19 and Trump?

The rocks are in the fog on the way to Ragged Island.
America is over.
And the dishwasher in the kitchen
Is issuing its warning
That the waves will sink the boat and the rocks are in the fog.

Employees at the beach resort are scooping up
Fetuses aborted on the pink sand.
The unborn look like jellyfish.
Living slime that sings and stings is what
I am.

John Malkovich, the thoughtful actor, in his role as Seneca,
Rats crawl out of their own assholes,
Turns to face the movie audience
And face America and the January 6th insurrection,
When monsters crawled out of their own assholes.

Remember, Seneca had been Nero's tutor.
Seneca was a rich man and a Stoic philosopher.
Seneca was a playwright
Famous for the horror, known to Shakespeare,
Of one play, called *Thyestes*, in particular.

Rats crawl out of assholes
And turn around to go back in.
A king sits down to a supper prepared by his brother,
Not knowing he's about to eat
A delicious stew of fatty meat

Made of his own small children.
What a ghastly stew,
Prepared by a brother he thought he knew,
Chunks of his children, now soft as goo, in the stew,
Each horrible bite delicious, too.

Imagine "Little Boy" and "Fat Man"—
The first atomic bombs—
Bullwhipping an explosive mob into a froth
To unhinge the U.S. Capitol and bring death
Under a radioactive mushroom cloud of dyed blond hair.

The mob bulges down Pennsylvania Avenue
Toward the Capitol.
The bullying bulk of President Donald Trump—
Nero of Mar-a-Lago—
Fucks them from behind like a dog.

IN MEMORY OF CLARE PEPLOE

The most beautiful woman who ever was
Is what the crematorium does.
The crematorium oven is the last one
Who gets to be with everything she is:
Wit, heart, lungs, voice, beauty, brain in an urn
They present you with for sprinkling the ashes around.
It is a fearful thing to love what death can touch.

So I take the elevator down
Instead of the staircase now.
No flying down the stairs, no more.
How rare to—
Once in a lifetime—
Meet someone who
Makes you stop and stare forever.

I'm sitting in a chair at a desk.
I'm walking down a street.
It's hot summer. It's cold winter. It's not nowhere.
I was a comer
Once. I walked around in a mummy case of glamour.
I coulda been a contender
Is the line I remember,

Instead of a bum, which is what I am.
Underneath the Harvard hoodie, it was me.
Tap tap tap tap . . . that's the computer keyboard,

Not the sound of a white cane and impaired sight.
I wake from a dream in which the three blond siblings
Who occupy the tall house in Belgravia's Chapel Street,
Two girls and a boy, eternal, immortals,

Are all still here
In their dazzling twenties, happily orphaned, that is to say
Both parents alive but keeping out of the way,
No parent around, a dream.
Getting up in the middle of the night
Is what you have to do sometimes if you write—
And you turn on the light.

BERNARDO BERTOLUCCI

A thousand years ago when we were young,
All the posh kids in London were spouting Mao.
Antonioni had done *Blow-Up*.
Posh kids in Paris were doing smack.
Godard was mouthing Mao.
Along came Bernardo.

I told Bernardo I regarded Aldo Moro
As the Abraham Lincoln of the Italian Republic,
Who, trying to find a compromise to save Italy,
Got kidnapped and murdered by the terrorist Brigate Rosse.
The Red Brigades were the equivalent of the assassin
John Wilkes Booth.

A small red Renault
Parked in Via Caetani near the Ghetto
Contained the bullet-riddled corpse of Moro and his
Compromesso storico—
Which terror on all sides
Didn't want alive.

Bernardo was more sympathetic than I was
To the drastic romance of the extremists.
I made a pilgrimage to the spot where they found
Moro's body stuffed in the trunk.
There was a plaque.
People stood on the sidewalk and wept.

The goddess Bernardo married
Was a muse for many, including Michelangelo Antonioni.
When *The Last Emperor* won nine Oscars,
Including for best picture,
Bernardo saluted what he called The Big Nipple of Hollywood
In his smiling little speech.

That lovely wicked smile!
Same with his voice—sly, mellifluous, sweet.
We talked politics, psychoanalysis,
Physiotherapists!
We talked about Rome and Todi, the East Hampton of Italy.
We talked bad backs and movies, bad-backery and poetry!

Bernardo had things wrong
With him and changed doctors all the time,
Changed medications constantly,
Always trying out
Some absolutely sure
New cure.

Two things in life are sure: there's always a new medicine
And cure, and always a new translation
Of the untranslatable.
Galassi marvelously translated Montale
But his Leopardi took on the impossible.
The sublimity who loved infinity can't be translated.

Bertolucci didn't disagree when we discussed
Pain leading to art over pasta in New York.
Leopardi was a cripple who spent his time on earth
Ascending from his ankylosing spondylitis
And railing against the iniquity
And decline of Italy.

Never deliver a script on time
If you want to be taken seriously!
Bernardo was teasing Mark Peploe and me
For working till dawn night after night
To finish *Out of the Blue*—
That never got made.

Birds were singing their eternal joy
Every morning when we went to bed,
Stinking of cigarettes and inspiration.
There we were in Florence,
A thousand years ago when we were young.
Leonardo da Vinci had painted nearby.

The great Italian filmmaker Bernardo Bertolucci
Has just this minute died of lung cancer in Rome.
It's the twenty-sixth of November, two thousand eighteen.
Finding it harder and harder to breathe,
He suddenly sighed,
And seemed relieved, and died.

ONE MISSOURI SENATOR

What's happened to Missouri?
It has a senator
Who looks like
Adolf Hitler
And likes himself enough
To *Sieg heil* the mirror.
He looks like a lobster.

The senator gestures approval
Of the rioters
At the U.S. Capitol
With a thumbs-up lobster claw and smile.
He thinks everything is going to be extreme right
MEGA MAGA by torchlight tonight
On Main Street America.

In the days of my youth,
I was young.
I kissed the scarecrow on the lips.
I rode my bicycle upside down.
I laughed my way through enemy lines
And played the violin
Till my blond curls darkened.

In the days of my youth,
When I was young,
I wanted a gun.
Bang bang boom boom
I was cowboys
Or sometimes I was Native Americans,
Or I was Nazis and Gestapo but Jewish.

How green St. Louis was
When I was young.
My button nose was always clogged
With heavenly fragrance.
I still dream of this St. Louis
Insufferable bliss of grass and trees
And that and this.

In Forest Park
There was a marvelous thing of glass
Called the Jewel Box, in which one was mostly
Immense and delirious with the perfume
Of flowers and plants
In a state of pre-psychedelic
Airborne invention.

THE BALLAD OF BAN THE BOMB

He wanted to meet as soon as possible,
Desperately wanted me to collaborate with him to fulfill
A years-overdue commission he had from the State of Israel.
He had in mind some sort of ban-the-bomb oratorio

That would have its premiere at the Knesset.
We met in summertime Central Park
In green glorious New York,
But was I interested?

And afterward he kissed me goodbye on the mouth,
Shock to a St. Louis boy,
The maestro bursting with genius and joy
While putting me into a Checker cab.

I was twenty-six,
The perfect age for vast ambition.
We were there to save civilization!
Robert Lowell had told him I might be interested.

The piece, but without me, became eventually
The *Kaddish* Symphony, but by then
Israel already probably (certainly) had the bomb.
Shalom.

Lowell had told him I was the best.
Once he heard that, Bernstein would never rest.
I liked the sweetness
Of being pursued by the maestro

From, so to speak, Maine to Mexico.
At eighty-five, I miss the sweetness
Of being pursued *sans cesse*
All over the East Coast, age twenty-six.

MIDNIGHT SKY WITH STARS

Dick Poirier, lead sled dog of our team,
Where do the dead go when they're gone?
And fireflies when they're done?
They go nowhere and that's where they're to be found.

Your death was (weren't you lucky!) years before
The victory of toothsome Trump.
Nor do you have to wear a mask
Every time you go outside

Because of course you've already died.
I'd love to hear you in your roaring mode
Denouncing vividly and lividly the Orange Toad—
Our president (the Donald)—

And his incredible regime of fraud.
I smile to think of you and how you got yourself
Cosmetically enhanced, not once but twice,
But "only to look better, not younger."

Long before the fervent vogue for cooking
Columns in *The New York Times*,
And endless, endless restaurant reviews,
You were sweet on life, you were meat and life,

At Café Luxembourg, which we adored,
Though the son of a Gloucester fisherman favored
All-American meatloaf over anything francophone.
You enjoyed America and were in love with America

And loved the Library of America
That embalms America on Bible paper
Whose literature sleeps on nothing but the best.
You've missed the dying gasps of the United States.

You died before the pandemic virus.
You've missed this year's pandemic election politics.
Twenty twenty is our annus horribilis,
To quote from one of your favorites, Queen Elizabeth.

It came upon a midnight clear,
Walking you from Lux your usual one block home—
But you couldn't even walk one block,
And that meant that the end was here.

And then you fell into the street
Out of a cab in front of your building's front door,
Just after talking about the magical
New York City Ballet/Balanchine miracle.

Dick Poirier, lead dog of our team,
Where do the deadydead go when they're gone?
And fireflies when they're done? I swear
They go somewhere and that's where they're to be found.

Emerson, Frost, Eliot, Shakespeare, Henry James.
Flashbulbs blinding the dark.
All that blinding light, all that lovely talk
Burst apart on the sidewalk.

THE AUTOBIOGRAPHY
OF SUNSHINE

The sidewalk is full of sunlight.
The street is full of sunlight.
Fare forward, amici!
Some citizens cross Broadway.
There's life on the other side.
When you wake up in the morning
With nothing to do, this is what you do.
You sit down.

You need to see a specialist
To lead you through
Your white man's mist.
White people
Need a team of specialists
For surgery to slit their racist wrists,
If such a procedure exists,
And sew the Union back together.

Mike Leonard is my friend and doctor.
Weill Cornell is my hospital.
I need a specialist
To lead me through my mist.
I need surgery
To slit each racist wrist
And press the starter button
To restart.

Swiftly moving pure-white enormous clouds
Against a pure-blue sky,
As if the huge clouds were white smoke
Trying frantically to escape
An enormous fire nearby.
The country is burning
Up Black people
And Covid is coming.

It's hard not to be dead!
It's hard to stay awake.
You fall asleep at your desk.
Your head falls toward your lap.
And then there's the matter of sex.
You fall off your tricycle, so to speak,
And are lifted into a bassinet
And start to forget.

Your study looks south.
You work until you don't
Which is when you go out.
You look at the man in the mirror,
A face the size of the moon.
There apparently are people
Who can't recognize faces.
Faces are as meaningless as feces.

It's really old outside.
The young woman is full of sunlight
And it shows in everything she does.
It's really old outside and cold outside and hot outside
On the Upper West Side
Where the ambulances and the firetrucks play
Up and down Broadway.
Home, home on the range!

I think highly
Of Mr. Andrew Wylie.
Home, home on the range.
Where seldom is heard
A discouraging word from my agent or my publisher.
The thing is to work every day, daily,
With gallons of time to work in
And the day luffs lightly like a sail.

The thing is to have a routine
And go from point to point
Touching every base
Before moving on to the next slit my racist wrists.
Every day I roar down Broadway
For ten blocks and back or more,
Barnes & Noble and back, one mile.
Slit my racist wrists. It's my constitutional!

Now it's nearly two o'clock.
Covid is coming.
They call me Sunshine at my diner.
Everyone thinks I am the finest and couldn't be finer.
I twirl on my seat at the counter.
Isaac Bashevis Singer, great white writer, in a suit and tie,
Lunched here with his wife until he died, either
Coming from his mistress or about to go to her.

IN VIENNA

The Lipizzaners of the Spanish Riding School
Are infinitely white stallions of magnificence like me.
I like the costume of the riders,
Especially the high black boots that cap the knee.

The Spanish Riding School is in Vienna.
Performances take place in the Winter Riding School.
Trainees learn to ride without reins or stirrups.
Just don't fall off is their Talmud and their shul.

Between Michaelerplatz and Josefsplatz
Inside the Hofburg in the central city
Is the exquisitely simple performance hall,
All quiet white and full of sunlight.

A large painted portrait of Emperor Charles VI
Hangs above the royal box.
Below it, whites and sunlight mix.
White riders manage white magnificence!

There are Nazis in Vienna and neuroses.
An astonishing collection of Titians lives here, too.
Freud worked in Vienna until the Nazis.
It's almost always better not to be a Jew.

THE CANTILEVERED
BUILDING

The apartment buildings on Broadway,
Including the new ones going up,
And there are many going up,
Are the trees I breathe,
Are the forest where I live.
The redskins are behind every boulder—
Only they're Black.

We're going back to nature.
We're giving up on city life.
The birds are whistling in the trees,
Or is that an Indian scout?
Branches crackle underfoot.
Our presence has been noted.
The forest floor is not our friend.

There's a cantilevered new building
On Broadway leaning out from itself
As it attempts to get finished
And get more mileage out of the zoning laws,
Or do I mean the building code?
Build yourself sky-high.
Hang out over yourself.

Central Park is ten thousand miles away.
It's three blocks away.
It's in the Amazon. It's in Paris.
America is over and over
Over.
Buildings are bleeding on top.
White man scalp savages.

THE ARIZONA INN

Tucson is boring but then
Joy is shattering.
The blue of the sky is where the visiting Blue Angels fly.
Almost everything in Arizona is true.

I'm an airplane taking off.
I'm an airplane landing.
I'm the Pima Air & Space Museum.
I'm Gate 11 at the little Tucson airport.

I'm landing and taking off,
I'm getting in and getting out and getting back.
The giant hairless cactus between my ears
Has probably been there for a million years.

But it's not just the saguaros that are prehistoric.
Many men in the old days here were *men*,
Most of whom had gone to Yale,
Some of them Rough Riders with Teddy Roosevelt

When Arizona was still a territory.
Acres of retired military planes in tidy rows
Sit in placid silent sunlit outdoor storage in their dotage
In the dry desert air.

I even liked Denison Kitchel,
Goldwater's radically right-wing campaign manager,
Another Arizona Yalie pal of my right-wing father-in-law—
Whose liberal half-brother, wonderful Jack Greenway,

Looked like Proust's idea of a glamorous cowboy
And spoke French urbanely with a lisp.
Jack owned and did many things,
And owned the Arizona Inn, where JFK had stayed.

Blue Angels do or die.
Blue Angels fill the ear and air and eye.
Blue Angels in the Tucson sky
Do precision flying upside down, which is why

F-15s from Davis-Monthan Air Force Base believe
In God and dive and dream.
The noise is deafening. Everyone is everything and screaming
Every woman is a king!

I'm at the glorious Sonoran hotdog stand
Next to the car wash
In front of the McDonald's, just off the highway,
And the very proud proprietor hands me my dog.

At the Arizona Inn I sink in,
Oasis in the Sahara for the weary Bedouin.
The blue-trim pink buildings are feminine.
The swimming pool and gardens are the same as love.

LUCKY DUCKY

I have an appointment with my cardiologist
On East End Avenue to take a stress test,
And afterward walk along John Finley Walk along the East River
Below that very grand apartment building at 10 Gracie Square
With a porte cochère
Where poor X recently leapt to her death
While looking out over the park and Gracie Mansion and the river.

I always recommend to the recently dead that they visit
The new Brooklyn—Brooklyn for the young!
Right now I am on the opposite
Side of the river on the Bowery
On my way to a little theater to watch
My nephew performing an autobiographical
Performance piece he wrote.

Alas, I won't fly to London to Mary-Kay's great birthday.
Mary-Kay, Happy Birthday!
It's not good to fly with pneumonia.
But what a bore. The moxifloxacin is hardcore.
I do my little stretching exercises on the floor.
You don't have to pay any attention to me anymore.
I have become someone to ignore.

It actually
Seems quite weird to be sick, and inappropriate, but I am.
It doesn't seem natural.

And it seems quite odd to be old.
What if it turns out I'm not!
I notice sometimes
I do feel a bit odd, however.

Nothing is more platitudinous than unhappiness.
I have a theory about getting over it.
Shelter Island on Long Island,
Between the South Fork and the North Fork,
You can reach by ferry from Sag Harbor or Greenport,
And by helicopter to East Hampton Airport
From your Manhattan heliport.

I fed the dog.
I've paid the maid.
I'm ready to go.
I lay down on the flo.
I don't feel like living no mo.
By the dawn's early light,
I will say good night.

The point in the age of Trump is to be rich,
And if you can't be, don't bother me.
Don't bother if you're not going to be serious—seriously.
The republic has already fallen apart and this is the subsequent empire
Falling apart.
Or has already.
You like my grammar?

The point in the age of Trump is to be rich enough to leap
From your triplex apartment's enormous terrace at dawn
To oblivion while enjoying the view.
Dawn opens its eye.
It's daytime all over again.
Nero ordered Seneca to kill himself.
All over the Roman Empire, the Roman Empire began to end.

This poem you're reading is the blanket of foam
The fire department lays down on the flames of Nero's Rome,
Which however has already burned down,
And separates screaming children from their weeping parents
And the other way round.
The performance piece is called *Lucky Ducky*,
An hour of hilarious mayhem.

THE BIG BEAK

A fellow everyone likes is crying in 33B
Which the handyman mopping the hallway hears.
The fellow's certainly not crying because he's happy,
And it makes the handyman feel crappy.

Elsewhere in the high-priced city but only blocks away
Someone else is going on.
It's hard to keep things straight.
This one is holding a gun.

Blood is running down the Uber driver's cheek.
He ran a red light.
Tank Gott, he missed the baby carriage!
Of course, she was talking on her phone at the same time.

There's nothing like the City Sublime
To blur and focus at the same time.
You have to blur and focus yourself
To get the empty out.

Listen. People are living and dying
Everywhere and crying
All over the world. They're trying.
They're dying.

When a young couple with lots of money
Moves into a large Park Avenue apartment they've bought,
The first thing they do before they move in
Is tear the distinguished old thing apart.

Do you remember out in the country in summertime St. Louis
Eating amazing fried chicken at the Green Parrot restaurant
Under the dreamy, blissful starry night sky?
There was a green parrot with a big beak in a cage.

HUCK FINN

Rafting down the Mississippi River,
With fishing poles fishing for their dinner,
Is the picture Jack and Archie Bowles offer,
Fishing at a pond in England with their father.

Even in the photograph,
You can smell lovely England summer in the air.
The photographer is their father, Alastair,
Teaching the kids, seven and nine, how to fish.

Once upon a time, when I was seven or nine,
There was a memorable sign
On the way to the swimming pool
At the Piping Rock Club in Locust Valley, New York:

NO DOGS OR CHAUFFEURS BEYOND THIS POINT
When I was seven or nine
And barefoot like Huck Finn
And brown as a violin.

THE SONGBIRD ON THE CROCODILE'S BACK

The man can't stay awake. He falls asleep.
It's noon, it's afternoon, repeatedly he falls in deep,
Seated at his desk or in an armchair, as if to try to write a poem meant
A flash flood of sleep and drowning on Parnassus in his tent,
Or something else equally not good.
The guy's completely gone and sawing wood,
Snoring and snorting—until one snort wakes him—
And where is he? he can't think where he is—which shakes him.

He's upside down and he can see
The parachute he's hanging from is tangled high up in a tree.
He passes out again and drools.
This apparently is one of the Muse's rules.
He hears the pleasant droning of the plane he jumped from flying away,
But he's in his study and it's the same day.
He's in his study now and here's his long-dead dog.
Jimmy, my sweety boy, my Jimmy, come back to me through the fog.

Musa, mihi causas memora . . . you know?
You've seen a baby lift its foot to suck its toe
And then go back to sleep for several years
And then wake up to find a whole nation in tears . . .
Multiple assassinations, Black and white, white and Black,
Chest covered with medals split open by a national heart attack.
Baby has grown up to be an outrage carrying a weapon.
He's graduated from West Point and found little babies to step on.

Liquid gold streams down the buildings all the way down Broadway
At sunset, after a perfect fall day in May, the sky so blue it made you say
Something had to be God to lead to this
Furious brilliance you wouldn't want to miss
By being dead, for example, or otherwise asleep.
He saw a man once start to weep
But stop himself in time,
Because crying for a certain sort of man is correctly considered a crime.

Look how the sky is turning beautiful black and blue,
Reminding us how the aftermath of pain can be beautiful and true.
The apartment lights before they go out come on.
Hours later it's dawn.
Narcolepsy is supposed to be the subject, but it really isn't the subject, nor
Is the man fleeing from a crime he committed in Ulan Bator.
He didn't cry in the hotel elevator.
He's not the Ulan Bator crying elevator satyr.

That didn't stop the girl with the eating disorder driving the car from crashing.
He comes to after the crash, as usual at his desk, splashing
His face with cold water from the nearby lake,
Though he's already thinking of the next move to make.
He'll move to Rio. He'll move to Napoli. He opens the study door.
He'll move to the little apartment on the second floor.
Every day alive is dawn.
The lights before they go out go on.

TRAVEL

Never been to Moscow.
Never wanted to go.
Never been to Belgrade.
Must be beautiful under the snow.

I've been cold in your arms
Kuala Lumpur
And nearby Tioman Island
Where I sweated and felt fever.

I liked Mexico City
But I was just a boy.
With my parents' money
I got myself a real matador's hat.

I liked Mumbai better
When it was called Bombay.
I liked Cavafy's poetry better
Even than motorcycles.

Debonair in Iran
I liked François Villon.
An agent of the shah
Tried to trick me into saying something

At a gorgeous dinner party in a tent
Two waiters to each guest.
Only the finest caviar
Only available to friends of the shah.

Ballade des pendus.
Ballade des dames du temps jadis.
I was shot at in Guatemala.
An earthquake in Bali.

At Ryōan-ji in Kyoto
Waiting for my mojo,
My heart didn't move.
My brain didn't move.

VICTORY

Shooting the movie of Joseph Conrad's *Victory*,
We swam in the South China Sea.
The producer said we could and should.
Starring Willem Dafoe as Heyst.

The guidebook sold at the resort's front desk
Told you fourteen kinds of venomous snakes
Come down from the jungle at dawn once a year
To lay eggs on the beach but don't be scared.

Stretched out on her beach towel getting a tan
Was imperturbable Janet, the movie's Best Boy,
While Willem screamed by on a jet ski like a madman,
Spewing a rooster tail of joy behind his splendor!

AT EIGHTY-SEVEN

I had a plan to race my motorcycle,
My racetrack-only factory Superbike racer,
Not meant for the streets of Manhattan,
Illegal river to river, *wap wap wap* WOW!
The sound of over a hundred miles an OW
At a very early morning hour to avoid any traffic,
Down the FDR Drive,
Up the West Side Highway to Spuyten Duyvil,

Snarl *suck suck suck* waaah
Up through the gears
At a hundred and thirty miles an ow-eh
Climbing the stone steps to the top of the sacred tao-eh
Having as a model the great French short film
C'était un rendez-vous of 1976 by Claude Lelouch,
Which ends up on top of Montmartre
After roaring through sleeping Paris.

Lelouch discovered there was
A brilliant new movie camera,
Not even on the market yet,
Small enough to hold fairly steady in a moving car.
It cost a fortune—but profits from his disgusting
Recent commercial success
(*A Man and a Woman*)
Would pay.

A whale is spouting—*thar she blows!*—
On a diving board above an empty swimming pool,
No water in the pool, though it's August, it's summer,
So balance, yes balance, don't fall, makes sense.
I'm springing up and down
On a swimming pool diving board,
Waving above my head the razor
And other things you need to start.

What's my lighthouse without the lighthouse keeper
Living in the lighthouse—the way it used to be—
And maintaining the lighthouse and the lighthouse light
While whales spout off Montauk Point?
I have a rendezvous with death
Is the title of my last breath.
I fling the car door open and you're there waiting
As soon as I reach the top.

A MISTY, RAINY DAY

The electric clock by the bed
Doesn't know any better than to tell the time,
Even when it's one minute to zero
And the cockroach comes out on stage
Innocently expecting applause.

Why am I asking you, you ask.
It's an open-coffin sort of
Torso and above
Or should we say a face resembling
Misty, rainy gauze?

Manhattan is in gauze because
The rainy, misty daze
Of not quite wide awake but almost reaching
For the day that's going off
In the alarm will for sure be wonderful and love.

WHEN *THE PARIS REVIEW* WAS IN PARIS

The next time I saw Paris
Her streets were lined with Arabs
Not wearing wine or flowers.
Notre-Dame on fire
Burned above the Seine.
The working class and students and women
Marched down the Haussmann boulevards
Quite properly protesting everything.

I was never ever Abélard
Except for that one day
Héloïse took off her leotard
And we began to pray.
And every medieval inch
We pushed out of our way
And got down to the croissants
They serve at Café de Flore.

God is the color of Molière.
The Champs-Élysées has turned brown,
Which has somehow to do with Islam.
French politicians call for more
Whorehouses but there is already
So much French culture and so
Many improbably beautiful *poules de luxe*
On daytime duty outside the Madeleine.

I'm a Lamborghini out of breath—
I.e., a former cheetah—
Remembering Eddy Morgan, Digby Neave,
And other heavy smokers in our tiny headquarters
In Rue Vernet,
Just off the Champs-Élysées,
Thumbing our noses at lung cancer
In the first year of Jack Kennedy's New Frontier.

ROME

What could be sweeter
Than the salt of an oyster
But you, dear,
When you open your shell?
When you open your shell
You're heaven with hair!

There are so many tourists.
How can so many tourists exist!
Down the Via del del del Babuino I go,
Down the Via del Babuino I row
Against the current
To Piazza del Popolo.

Her mother was a seamstress
And didn't love her father.
Her mother was a seamstress
But they lived in Parioli,
Where everyone is rich.
She wore clothes her mother made

Better than
The rich kids wore
Who had their weekend houses
Where she never went.
Smarter than the others are,
She's risen up and up and up all her life.

STREET FAIR FOR BOB KERREY
ON HIS EIGHTIETH

Once upon a time, I saw the bellhop
Running toward me
With a message
Telegram for you sir

I am going there in case you have forgot
Mussolini got the trains to run on time
And I am going where
Il Duce Mussolini

Was the fascist leader of an Italy
In case you have forgot that
Once upon a time there was once
A real place called in English Italy

Once upon a time, I saw the bellhop
Running toward the senator
With a message
Telegram for you sir

The rickshaw
Has got rickety
Arthritically for two old
White men

The shame
And embarrassment
Of being olden
And having crinkled skin tissue-paper thin

The Medal of Honor one is
A Nebraska Cornhusker
They used to be called Bug-eaters reborn
With a gun in Vietnam in gory glory

Thus Ben and la Clara a Milano
Sang Ezra Pound softly
About the hysterical
Brutality

We hung the corpses of Mussolini and Clara Petacci
His mistress upside down
In the center of the town
And went back to Harvard

YOUTH

Bourbon and scrambled eggs for breakfast
Upstairs in their dowdy suite at the old Boston Ritz
As guests of Brahmin old-fart trustees
Of *The Harvard Advocate*, 1955 or maybe 1956.

I was the magazine's Pegasus, the literary editor.
I knew these sophisticates were hicks.
I was from St. Louis—nineteen years old.
Ezra Pound was my movie star.

Chintz daylight filled the room
And the deep mahogany bourbon we sipped.
Edible scrambled eggs
We ate while we got ripped.

We children wore the beautiful bourbon
Like a beautiful turban.

TUMP

It's raining hard,
Big raindrops the color of mustard.
Above them, if you can believe it, there's a rainbow
Aching over the street and
Connecting rat with rot.
Tell me life isn't only
The projects and slums
And endless homeless begging bums.
It numbs!
Just direct my feet but be discreet
To the sunny side of the street but be discreet.
From the rainy side
You see the other side,
Baskets of sunlight on their sidewalk,
Where the rats eat,
While the rain rains down un-light here, dear.
I fear the coming election will be
The end of American good.
America is having a makeover with
Cancer-and-financier Tump.
I mean crook.
The cat has jumped out of the fiddle
And is scratching our eyes out
Which itch with disbelief
That it's come down to this red-hot skillet, hot-shit creep,
Crook, dope. Tump.

MOTO POETA

Now and again, I feel a throb
Passing through my body like a sob,
Which is both painless and of no consequence,
Like a wave washing up on a beach,
But which feels like or prompts the thought
It may be the beginning of a stroke,

But probably it is just the irregular heartbeat
Of atrial fibrillation (AFib)
Or starting up a reluctant motorcycle.
The word *throb* makes it sound
As if it had to do with sex.
The word *motorcycle* means it does.

Jeff Nash is starting up a Ducati Supermono
At Advanced Motor Sports,
His splendid shop in Dallas,
Ducati motorcycles all around, all red, all beautiful,
Ducatis as far as the eye can see,
Each small and perfect as a ladybug.

The little Supermono
With a splash of mustard color on its tail is arguably
The most beautiful.
The single-cylinder motor needs a separate
Starter cart to start it.
This is a race bike, which means without a starter or lights.

The starter cart has a wheel that rotates pressed
Against the raised rear tire of the Supermono,
With the clutch lever pulled in, which when Nash releases it
Blat Blat Blat ejaculation
And then the explosion smooths.
The music makes some people

Listening to the exquisite
Concert actually cry.
There is a company called
Keyboard Motorcycle Shipping
That, not so long ago, only
Transported nine-foot concert grand pianos

And racing motorcycles,
That was their only cargo,
Music flowering into power.
Nash is what
Used to be called in the movies
The strong silent type,

A kind, courteous, muscle-bound gentleman with brains,
Very smart, very honest,
Very old-fashioned in his politeness,
Very smart, very honest, very old-fashioned good manners.
I admire him for all these things,
And for being ruthlessly capable of running the competition

Off the track.
I have four motorcycles at his shop.
His wife, Toni, I admire as well.
In Sag Harbor, New York,
Water all around,
Where many moons ago I dwelled,

Oh what a lovely little place, far from boiling Dallas,
Country roads where I rode my motorcycles, catapulted
At a hundred miles an hour midair
By the rippling, bucking Old Montauk Highway,
Which you enter after Amagansett,
Roller-coasting high enough

To see the nearby blue eye of the ocean.
In Sag Harbor, New York,
Water on three sides,
Lives Jason Epstein, ninety years old.
He was my first publisher
And was somewhat sinister,

And spoke in a sinister whisper,
But was a man of surpassing charm.
He read the manuscript of my book *Final Solutions* overnight
Which had been involved in a widely publicized scandal,
Had won a prize that was then taken away
After I had declined to accept the prize anyway

And all the judges had resigned.
Jason was ready to publish it in his Looking Glass Library
Series of children's books,
Unperturbed by the legal threats,
Which had frightened off the others.
We were having fun and Bennett Cerf,

Jason's boss, the head of Random House, went along,
Pointing up at the glowering cathedral next door
And Cardinal Spellman's silky power there,
Which leased Random House its space below.
"That fairy is going to throw me out of here
Because of you, Fred!"

Bennett is long dead.
Jason, we are both getting on.
Once, we were out on Jason's boat with our wives,
On our way to Block Island,
With our friend the novelist John Marquand
Who wrote under the name John Phillips

Because he was the son of the novelist John Marquand,
All of us hung over from the night before at George's,
And under the heatstroke summer sun
Jason ran us aground on a sandbar
And we were stuck in that watery hot hell of Long Island August,
And I had to get down in the water

And tow the big boat by its hawser off the sandbar,
A young man pulling a yacht
In the middle of Long Island Sound,
Which surely looked odd
With deep water all around.
I saw a photograph of a woman I didn't know

In a family scrapbook my granddaughter
Had put together for a school assignment.
It was my mother.
That can't be my mother.
Here was this vastly old lady
Facing the camera unsmiling.

My mother's blue-eyed schizophrenia plus electroshock
Had always kept her lovely skin unlined.
The unlined woman of my memory and fantasy apparently
Had turned into a raisin while I wasn't looking,
Which I too must be turning into.
A wrinkled mummy of my beautiful mommy

Goes skipping down the street
With a child's balloon on a string
Gaily bouncing along above her head.
In the balloon is my father,
Imprisoned in helium,
Who loved her.

The stars at night are big and bright
Deep in the heart of Texas.
They squeak and flap.
They swoop and shriek.
I struggle to bench-press the United States
Up off my chest.

Halfway between the twin ends of the barbell,
Halfway between diarrhea and constipation,
Lifting the Trump White House off my chest,
Here I am, with my harem of motorcycles, in Dallas, Texas,
Lifting the White House off my chest,
Lifting the roof off to let the bats out.

I lift the roof off the White House
To let the spiders out for their walk.
They walk and talk off the record.
They spin their sticky.
They get into your eyes and your mouth.
I'm not taking them up on it.

I take five different pills every morning who once took none,
A happy man on whom the sun is going down
Every dawn.
Dallas boils in August.
Flames leap off the Ducatis in the air-conditioned showroom.
They're silently ready to be alive.

I have a Ducati 999 F05 racer, dubbed
Moto Poeta by the factory race-department mechanics,
Who knew they were making it for a poet,
A motorcycle that twice tried
To catch fire with the alarmed rider astride,
Whose poet private parts nearly fried.

The cattle are metal
That stampede down the highway
In the stun-gun heat
Of morning rush hour Texas August.
In the hotel lobby where we're meeting,
We freeze to death in brutal Texas air-conditioning.

A man taking a blood thinner
To reduce the chance of stroke
Had better not race his 999
Down the final straight
At the Circuit of the Americas
Here in the Lone Star State

Because if he crashes
He won't be able to stop bleeding.
Lee Harvey Oswald, not far from our hotel, still
Steadies his rifle in the open window
Of the Texas Book Depository, still getting ready to kill
President John F. Kennedy when the motorcade drives by.

Jeff and Toni
Lead our party on our last night to a friend's restaurant
With a race car and motorcycles
And an airplane on display inside,
And there's even a one-person submarine
In an enormous oblong fish tank

Where magnificent fish swim about.
We sit at a long table
And tell each other the story
Of our steaks and lobsters,
Of our foie gras and Sauternes,
And the story of our glory,

And tell the poor outside the restaurant,
Tell the homeless all around us in the darkness,
That we couldn't stop until we stopped,
Ten thousand cartons through the years,
Three packs a day because we were fools:
Unfiltered Camels, Gauloises, Gitanes, and Kools.

I notice the wretched.
I mention the homeless.
I stride down the sidewalks where the homeless live
Who are ill and unable to stand and love.
I stride down the street,
My heart in AFib.

Motorcycles are what I'm made of,
That start and go fast and don't crash and don't end,
And that go faster than that and faster.
And the poems are like dogs that stand up
On their hind legs and bark
To get your attention.

I can remember the overwhelming breasts of Betsy Green,
Like some fertility goddess in the Ajanta Caves,
Where forty years ago in New York
I feasted and drank.
I can remember the bitter taste and stink
Of my ecstatic smoker's saliva on them, worshipping.

I can remember
That as you enter the harbor you hear
The buoy clanging
Through the fog.
Bong, bing, clang, ding, the buoy sings,
Rocking back and forth, lifted on wings.